Looking back at
Swansea

First published in Great Britain in 2008 by
Bryngold Books Ltd.,
Golden Oaks, 98 Brynau Wood, Cimla,
Neath, South Wales, SA11 3YQ.
www.bryngoldbooks.com

Typesetting, layout,
editing and design
by Bryngold Books

ISBN 978-1-905900-08-4

Printed and bound
in Wales by
Gomer Press,
Llandysul, Ceredigion.

Looking back at
Swansea

By David Roberts

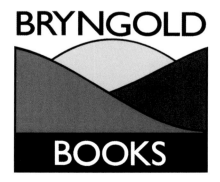

BRYNGOLD

BOOKS

Pictures please!

If you would like to play a part in recording the history of your area by contributing photographs to the next Swansea nostalgia book please telephone 01639 643961 or e-mail bryngold@btinternet.com to find out the ways in which you can do this. We would be delighted to hear from you. All photographs — black and white or colour — of people, places, events, streets, buildings, schooldays and sport are considered whatever their age, subject or format. They are all promptly returned. Also, if you have missed any of the previous books why not contact us now. additionally, check out our website address www.bryngoldbooks.com for details of other local nostalgia books.

Contents

Foreword

The pace of life in the 21st Century means that change envelopes us faster than ever. All too often it is possible to forget favourite haunts, familiar places and people we once met on a daily basis.

Thankfully, David Roberts has been there for more than a decade now to help refresh memories of the way we were in days gone by. He has provided a delightful series of pictorial nostalgia books that have grown into an easily accessible community archive for Swansea, something to which few other locations can lay claim.

Our city should be proud of the results of the picture gathering of just one man. And though he constantly reminds people that this is their book and that it flourishes only by the keenness of everyday folk to share their photographs, it could not happen without his diligence and determination.

Looking Back at Swansea is a special book that is a worthy addition to the collection that has appeared before. It is a unique photographic record of Swansea, its people, places and indeed all our lives. Much more than that, it reflects the changing social scene of our own special part of the world.

Every edition of this wonderful series of books bridges the generations and brings enormous pleasure as families share memories of times past. From the moment the pages of this book are opened to the time when the cover is closed it is difficult not to marvel at the images of the way Swansea once was. The book's fresh compilation of pictures says a great deal about our lives and the communities in which we live. I wish David well with this his 11th Swansea publication and on behalf of everyone salute his efforts and hope that this annual delight will continue for many years to come.

Councillor Gareth Sullivan
Lord Mayor of the City & County of Swansea
2008-09

A changing scene

Walk around Swansea today and at almost every turn you will be confronted by evidence of a vibrant city, building for the future. As with most other locations, change is something that down the decades occurred at a far more leisurely pace. Today however, familiar landmarks can vanish and new ones appear almost in the blink of an eye.

It is not difficult then to understand how modern Swansea can appear quite different to that depicted on the pages of *Looking back at Swansea*. Here instead is a guide to the way its streets and communities once were — and not so long ago at that.

Look closely and it is easy to spot changes, not only in the fabric of the area, but in its social trends too. The way butchers for example, once hung huge carcases of meat outside their stores; or the now vanished tobacconist shops that ministered to the needs of smokers; the multiplicity of pubs that existed on the streets; or the lack of traffic on them. In the docks too, quaysides that once pulsated with the comings and goings of a multiplicity of cargoes, now reverberate to the noise of new housing and offices being born.

Many will look at the pictures in this book with a heavy heart and a moist eye, but change is what helps our city thrive. Keeping alive the memory of the way it once was has become the role of all those who contribute to these books. Long may they — and Swansea — flourish.

David Roberts,
2008.

Appreciation

Our thanks are due to the Lord Mayor of Swansea, Councillor Gareth Sullivan, for his kind foreword to *Looking Back At Swansea,* a book that would not have been possible without the support of people from far and wide who have shared their pictures from the past to produce a fascinating record for future generations.

We are once again indebted to Ray & Dorothy Lewis of Solihull, for their continued support; Alan Williams, Roy Kneath, David Beynon, Bernard Morris, Rev Roy Bowen, Steve Phillips, Colin Andrew, the late Rev. R Alan Evans, Hilary Evans, Alan Jones, John and Marian Murphy, Dennis Spinks, Bernard Humphreys, John and Barbara Southard, John Jones, Roger Trollope, Julie Bennett, Hazel Rees, Terry & Joy Osborne, TB Harris, Julie Jones, Marjorie Ball, Jodie Jones, Pam Evans, Sandra Hayden, Phil Davies, Mrs T Fossey, Pauline Tancock, John Williams, May Strawbridge, Clive Cockings, David & Eluned Govier, Dolores Ramos Morgan, Barry Griffiths, Robin Wayne, Julian Hoskins, Keith Taylor, Cliff Dawson, Don Roberts, Betty Matthews, Gaye Mortali, David Lile, Bernard Thomas, Hilary Isaac, the late Dennis Scanes, Grahame Michael-James, Richard Baglow, Rita Lewis, Bill Barton, Julie Cole, Kathryn Owens, Mike Highfield, Roger and Julia Phillips. Thanks are also due to Anthony Isaac, Neil Melbourne and the staff of Gomer Press.

Last, but by no means least I must once again pay tribute to my wife Cheryl, without whose support, encouragement and involvement, none of these books would have appeared.

Chapter 1

A maritime panorama, looking south across the River Tawe, Swansea Docks and the bay beyond on February 28, 1985. Sainsbury's store is still under construction.

On the
Streets

St Helen's Road in the early 1900s. The tracks curving to the right led into the tramway depot. The Crown Court building is to the right today.

The tramway terminus, High Street, near its junction with College Street, 1910. The street was a honeypot for shoppers then. The terminus remained until 1912 when Castle Street was widened.

A fascinating view of High Street. The Mackworth Hotel, complete with ornate metalwork frontage, is on the left hand side 1910.

Parking outside your favourite Oxford Street store was rarely a problem in 1914. The Empire and Carlton Theatres are on the right hand side.

Crowds throng the pavement in Castle Street, 1918. Perhaps they were waiting for a tram.

Looking eastwards along De-La-Beche Street towards The Laurels, 1927. Dynevor School is just visible on the right. The properties behind the fencing were demolished to make way for an extension to the school which was completed in 1929.

A steam ship heads for the open sea as crowds enjoy a Sunday stroll along the West Pier, 1904.

Looking across the impressive floral clock at Victoria Gardens to Swansea Guildhall behind, late 1930s.

Looking into Alexandra Road from High Street, 1930. The railings in the centre surrounded an underground public convenience.

Buildings tower over the still-cobbled Strand, late 1920s.

A single deck tram car passes over the River Tawe's New Cut bridge, 1932.

1917

1904

1984

1926

1920

Down the years in Wind Street

1930

1910

1905

1976

The War Memorial, on the promenade near St Helen's sports ground, 1924.

The entrance to the Empire Theatre, Oxford Street, early 1930s.

The impressive council chamber at Swansea Guildhall, 1936.

Looking eastwards along Orange Street from its junction with Church Street, September 8, 1959.

Looking across Castle Gardens in the early 1960s. Morsmith Motors is on the left. The Evening Post then occupied the former Post Office and alongside are the remains of Swansea Castle.

Looking up the Kingsway towards the roundabout, early 1960.

A ship's lifeboat high and dry near part of the Weaver's flour mill, December 1963. Behind it a goods train can be seen on the high level railway line. The bus in the background is an AEC Renown Bridgemaster double decker supplied to South Wales Transport as a demonstrator and bought by the company in 1958. It was used mainly on the city's east side routes.

The Boots the Chemist store dominates this view across Castle Gardens in the late 1960s. Fast food restaurant McDonalds now occupies part of the building.

College Street, looking towards Woolworth's High Street store, 1963. The building is now occupied by Argos. The chimneys on the right were part of the Strand electricity generating station.

Industrial dereliction on the North Dock site, 1965.

A tank engine hauls wagons of timber towards the South Dock, October 1959. The rail line was sandwiched between the road and buildings alongside. Behind the bus is the Seamen's home.

Houses in Kensington Crescent at its junction with Catherine Street, 1946. This is now called St Helen's Avenue. Keatings garage is visible to the left.

Western Street looking towards Singleton Street, late 1960s.

The Evening Post building which dominated Adelaide Street, January 28 1968.

Looking down High Street into Castle Street, late-1950s.

This was the panoramic view from Kilvey Church, 1967.

The Cardigan House shop of ladies and gents fashion outfitters Sidney Heath at the junction of Wind Street and Caer Street, early 1930s. The shop was destroyed in the Three Nights Blitz.

Buildings in Alexandra Road, October 1971. On the right is the gated entrance to the arcade that stretched from here into High Street.

Traffic heads eastwards along Quay Parade, early 1970s.

Removal of the railway bridge that crossed the lower end of Wind Street, 1966.

A city panorama from Kilvey Hill, early 1970s.

Construction work underway on New Cut bridge, 1965.

The St Thomas entrance to Swansea Docks, with the Norwegian Church on the right, 1972.

The Slip bridge, late 1960s.

Oystermouth Road, late 1960s.

A hazy view along Oystermouth Road with one of the gasometers of Swansea gasworks clearly visible and on the right was the former Mumbles Railway depot, 1975.

St Helen's Road at its junction with Oystermouth Road, late 1960s.

Mount Pleasant Hospital and, below it, Swansea Institute of Higher Education, 1990. On the far left is Swansea Docks. Many of the terraced homes here have a bird's eye view of the city below.

Salubrious Passage,
linking Wind Street and
York Street, 1976.

**Green Dragon Lane, running between
Wind Street and the Strand, 1967.**

Pedestrians and traffic in Princess Way, mid-1970s.

Contractors topping out the marina-side Marriott Hotel, late 1980s.

A close-up of Swansea Museum from the top of BT tower, 1985. Early construction work on the marina-side flats and apartments can be seen behind.

Looking eastwards across the former North Dock towards St Thomas and Kilvey Hill, 1985.

Work in progress on the construction of the sea wall on the beach in front of Swansea Marina, late 1970s.

A mid-1980s rooftop panorama looking seaward from the top of the BT tower.

A view seawards across the River Tawe barrage shortly after completion, 1988.

A view across Swansea riverside during demolition of Weavers flour mill, 1984. Built by Charles Henebeque in 1897, it was Europe's first re-inforced concrete building.

The promenade at Swansea Marina, 1989.

Looking up the lower Swansea Valley from the top of the BT tower, February, 1985.

Argyle Chapel, St Helen's Road, shortly before it was badly damaged by fire on August 5, 2001. The building was later refurbished as an apartment block.

The former Swansea Guildhall, Somerset Place in 1990 before it was restored as the Dylan Thomas Centre.

The River Tawe barrage viewed from its seaward side, 2001.

Looking across the former North Dock area towards High Street, during the building of High Street multi storey car park, 1980s. St Thomas School is on the right.

The remains of Swansea Castle stand as firm as ever while the much newer BT tower block receives a facelift, 1989.

The Dylan Thomas Centre, Sainsbury's supermarket and a man-made island, constructed by Swansea Sub Aqua Club members, in the River Tawe to accommodate breeding ducks, 1993.

Work underway on road improvements at the junction of The Kingsway and Princess Way, 2006. The former pedestrian underpass was filled in. College Street is in the background.

Chapter 2

Members of various church youth clubs gathered in the grounds of Church House, St Helens Road, Swansea, 1944.

Faces and
Friends

A family gathering outside a house in Trebanos, Swansea Valley, 1920.

Rev Leslie Norman surrounded by members of the congregation and choir of St John's Church, Hafod, 1945.

These Swansea business people and their partners were gathered together at a New Year's Eve party, 1930.

The junior and senior sections of the Red Cross group at St Jude's Church, Mount Pleasant, 1938.

Staff of the Albert Hall cinema and their families on a day out to Porthcawl, September 8, 1946.

Some of the members of Christchurch Youth Club, Oystermouth Road, at Pwll Ddu, 1945.

Helpers at a Christmas Fair held at Terrace Road Presbyterian Chapel, 1959.

Members of St Thomas Church Sunday School, October 1963.

Some of those who helped organise the 1966 Christmas Fair at Terrace Road Presbyterian Chapel.

Civic dignitaries accompany Prince Charles as he visits Swansea on the post-Investiture tour during which he conferred City status on the former County Borough, August 1969.

The Rev FT Davies receives a celebratory gift during a party held to mark his retirement from Terrace Road Presbyterian Chapel, early 1970s.

A meeting of the Swansea branch of the Friends of the Gideon Society, early 1970s.

A group of Swansea Telecomm women enjoy a night out at Christmas, 1982.

Three Alcoa employees enjoy a drink during a safety evening at The Surf House restaurant, Bracelet Bay, 1977. The event was paid for by the company for safety target achievement.

Staff of Robin Wayne Florist's, Caer Street, with popular Grand Theatre pantomime star, Windsor Davies, late 1970s.

Members of Bishopston Ladies Lifeboat Guild meet HRH the Duke of Kent, during a special function at Mumbles Pier, February 1980.

Members of Darwin's Squash Club, Morriston, relax after taking part in a left-handed squash championship, during the early 1980s.

Riders in the British Heart foundation charity cycle run around Gower, 1987.

Employees at the BT Tower block, The Strand, say farewell to Leighton Rice, one of their colleagues, 1990.

Archbishop of Canterbury Dr Rowan Williams with members of Mumbles Community Council after they conferred the Freedom of Mumbles on him at a special ceremony, 2002.

Three members of 20th Swansea and 1st Morriston Scout Group were presented with their Queens Scout certificates at a special awards evening, 2000. Seated from left are Richard Jones, Jonathan Roberts and Ian Harris. Standing (from left) are: District Commissioner HB Weaver, Area Commissioner Anne Harris; Lord Lieutenant of Glamorgan, Robert Hastie and Swansea Lord Mayor, Robert Lloyd with Mayoress Val Lloyd.

The civic opening of Banbury's TV shop, The Kingsway, 1959.

Swansea Cub Scout leaders training at Gilwell Park, early 1970s, some of them came from Mumbles.

The Lord Mayor of Swansea, Susan Jones, at Oystermouth Infants School to mark its centenary, 1978.

Members of the Sisterhood at Hill Congregational Chapel, North Hill during a special presentation to one of their officers who was retiring, 2006.

A group, including ministers and lay preachers, gathered to celebrate the anniversary of the URC Chapel, North Hill, early 1960s.

Swansea Sea Cadets and Sea Rangers go through their paces watched by a group of Italian Guides at the South Dock basin, 1949.

Chapter 3

Looking up Trewyddfa Road, Landore, mid-1970s. Morris Castle remains are visible on the top left.

Around the
Districts

Woodfield Street, Morriston, 1910. It was a much quieter thoroughfare then.

Cottages at Bryntywod, near Llangyfelach, early 1900s.

Tirdeunaw, early 1900s. Tirdeunaw School is on the right and Caersalem Chapel is in the distance.

Martin Street, Morriston, late 1920s.

Glanbryddan Avenue, Uplands, under a blanket of snow, 1910.

Woodfield Street, Morriston, 1911.

Trafalgar Stores, Carmarthen Road, Fforestfach, puts out the flags to salute the Silver Jubilee of King George V and Queen Mary, 1935. Above, store owner Gladstone Williams, dispenses milk to a customer outside his store in the same year.

A queue for bread outside the Uplands bakery of D H Strawbridge, during wartime 1943.

Rectory Road,
Llanmadoc, 1925

The huts and bathers at
Langland Bay, August 3, 1983.

Memories of
Gower

Porteynon 1990.

A view of the Dunns,
Mumbles, 1970-71.

A flock of sheep block the road
at Rhosilli, August 15, 1979.

Pony exhibitors at
the Gower Show,
August 2, 1979.

A view across Limeslade Bay, August 1966.

Southgate, 1967.

Girl Guides at their summer camp, Oxwich, 1930.

Fabian Street, Port Tennant and coal yard railway sidings that were cleared to make way for the construction of Fabian Way, mid-1950s.

Cwmdonkin Park, Uplands, 1935.

Swansea canal looking down the valley towards Landore railway viaduct, late 1950s.

Properties in Balaclava Street, St Thomas, that were swallowed up by the construction of the Fabian Way dual carriageway, 1962.

The Vale of Neath Arms, Port Tennant, January, 1964.

Railway arches at the junction of
Thomas Street and Fabian Way,
St Thomas, 1968.

Gabalfa Road, Sketty,
in the snow,
February 9, 1969.

Windmill Terrace,
St Thomas, July, 1969.

A View of the Hafod and Morfa works sites from White Rock, 1983.

Calland Street, Plasmarl, 1985.

A wet day at Sketty Cross, 1990.

De La Beche Road, Sketty, 1990.

A view of Swansea east side from Mayhill, April 26, 1994.

Playing fields at Morfa during the early 1980s, before construction of the Morfa athletics stadium which eventually gave way to the Liberty Stadium complex.

Looking eastwards from Wern Fawr Road, Port Tennant, September 1990. The cooling towers of BP Chemicals, Baglan Bay complex can be seen in the background.

Delhi Street, St Thomas, in the snow, 1978.

Gors Primary School, Townhill, 1985.

A view of Llwynderw House, which became Llwynderw hospital annexe, just off Mumbles Road, West Cross, 1983. It was later demolished to make way for a housing scheme.

The Imperial Hotel, Neath Road, Plasmarl, mid-1980s.

Chapter 4

The Welsh Touring Choir, based at Waunarlwydd, 1911.

Proud to Perform

The choir of St Mary's Church, Swansea, on an outing to Llandrindod Wells, 1920.

A group of pupils at Hafod Junior School dressed to take part in a Christmas pageant, mid-1920s.

Participants in a Christmas play staged at Oakleigh House School, early 1940s.

Madame Stockton's Dancing Troupe from Overland Road, Mumbles, during a performance of pantomime Dick Whittington in an old British Legion tin shack at Oystermouth 1950.

The cast of Jan of Windmill Land, a production by Clyne Sunday School members in the Vivian Hall, Blackpill, 1950.

A concert party formed by members of St David's Roman Catholic Church, during a performance at the Llewellyn Hall, 1953.

The full cast, officers and committee of Swansea Amateur Operatic Society on the evening of the producer's arrival for their performance of The Student Prince at the Empire Theatre, 1956.

Participants in the summer show staged by New Siloh Chapel, 1958.

Swansea Amateur Operatic Society members during their successful 1958 production of Oklahoma at The Grand Theatre, 1959.

The cast and back stage crew of the pantomime Aladdin staged at the Grand Theatre, 1964. Star of the show was Vince Eager.

The Outer Limits, at the Cellar Club, Morriston, 1964. The line up included Gilbert and Fred Tancock, guitars; Dave Myland, vocalist; Barry Evans guitar and Raymond Thomas, drums.

Swansea comedian Dave Swann with the cast of the Grand Theatre pantomime Jack and the Beanstalk, 1967.

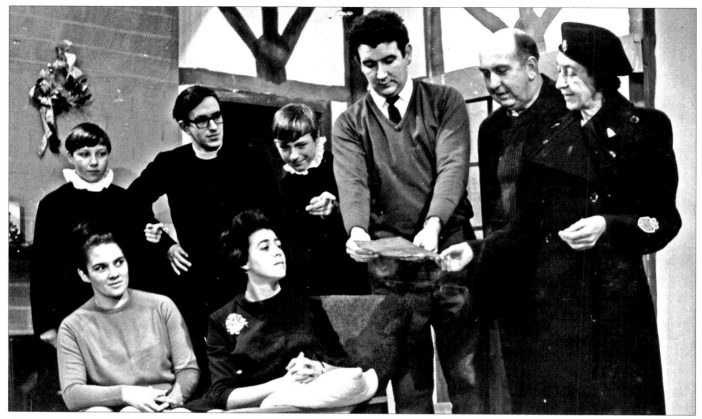

Captured during rehearsals are some of those who took part in a play entitled Fools' Paradise, and staged by members of St Michael's Church, Manselton, 1968.

Younger members of the congregation of Carmarthen Road United Reformed Church, Greenhill, who took part in a Nativity Play, 1981.

Members of the Dubensky School of Dance, 1976.

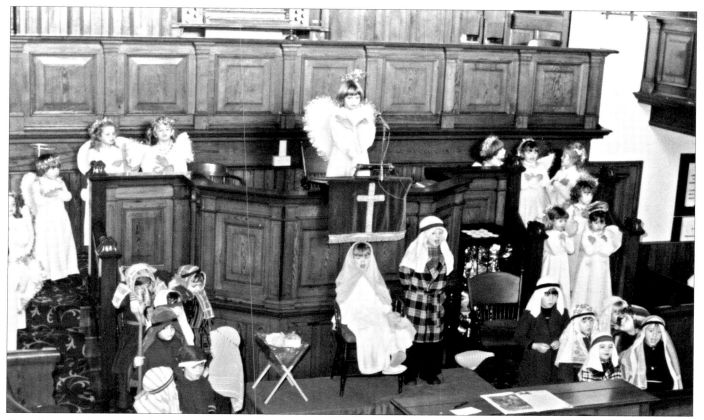

Gendros Primary School Nativity play, Christmas, 1979.

The cast of a play staged at St Thomas church hall, including Fred Secombe, brother of the late Sir Harry Secombe, 1971.

These were the youngsters who took the parts of the Von Trapp children in a production of The Sound of Music by St Thomas Church, mid-1980s. They are pictured with one of the organisers.

The choir, orchestra and cast of Penlan School's performance of Tom Sawyer with Miss Love at the piano, 1986.

The male chorus of The Gondoliers, performed at the Taliesin Theatre by Uplands Arts Club, 1994.

Girls from the Hazel Johnson School of Dancing, mid-1980s.

Chapter 5

Girls of Swansea Sea Cadet Corps at Singleton Park, 1949.

When we were Young

A group of youngsters enjoy the sun and sand on Swansea Beach, 1962.

Anticipation, excitement and delight combine for these children as they open their gifts on Christmas morning 1965.

The Fairfield Terrace gang, 1953.

Two Townhill brothers enjoy some time with their dad, 1950.

Some of the angels who took part in the Nativity play at Terrace Road Primary School, 1969.

Swansea and District Cubs during a sandcastle building competition on Swansea Beach, 1983.

Youngsters of Milton Terrace, Mount Pleasant, enjoy a traditional game of skipping, 1988.

Jamie Trollope, aged three, at the wheel of his dad's confectionery delivery van, 1973.

Youngsters at play on the climbing frame in Maesteg Park, St Thomas, late 1970s.

An aunt and her nephew inspect the two galvanised baths hanging up in the back yard of a typical Swansea home in Greenhill, 1943.

Children of Wimmerfield, Killay, at Caswell Bay, with their parents, 1946.

Members of the 16th (Swansea) St Gabriel's Scout troop outside St Gabriel's Church, Bryn Road with Father Webster, priest in charge and visiting Scouts, 1940s.

This car was made by Mr Trevor Davies who was a woodwork teacher and grandfather of the writer Russel T Davies, 1938.

Members of the 42nd Fforestfach Scout troop at their Carmarthen Road headquarters, 1984.

Coco the Clown surrounded by some of his young Swansea fans, 1964.

Two young Sketty sisters make the most of the snow in February 1978.

Whatever your age there was a way of getting around in 1936 Swansea.

Chapter 6

Colourful Days

Looking down on Swansea Castle from the top of the nearby BT tower, mid-1970s..

The tide was out when this picture of the River Tawe was taken during the winter of 1972. The building of the Tawe Barrage downstream meant that it is a view seldom seen today. The hillside terraces of St Thomas are on the right.

A close-up view towards Port Tennant and Danygraig from the top of the BT tower, 1985. Much of the foreground has now been taken up by the sprawling SA1 development.

New Cut bridge over the River Tawe and St Thomas railway bridge 1985. The Norwegian Church is visible on the right.

Looking westward towards the South Dock and the sea, 1984.

**Rotherslade Bay and the
Osborne Hotel, August 3, 1983.**

**Waves crash against the rocks
of Bracelet Bay, Mumbles, 1982.**

Three Cliffs Bay, August 4, 1979.

Looking across the rooftops of Mumbles towards the pier, 1969.

Work underway on road improvements at the junction of The Kingsway and Princess Way, Swansea, 2006.

The impressive timbered facade of buildings in Caer Street, 1971.

High Street, mid-1960s.

One of the colourful floats that took part
in Southgate Carnival parade, July 1971.

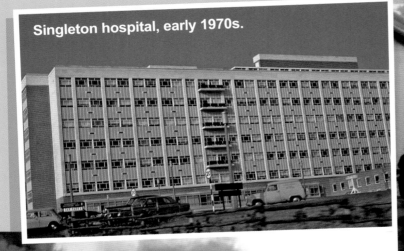

Singleton hospital, early 1970s.

BEDFORD

HWN 23W

Firemen fight to bring
a blaze at the South
Dock factory of
Spontex, early 1990s.

UNED GYNNAL

A Frozen Pond at
Singleton Park,
January 4, 1970.

Traffic on Fabian Street on the east side of the River Tawe, 1958. The remains of St Thomas Station are in the centre.

A Diesel Multiple Unit train heads out of Swansea towards Cockett tunnel, late 1970s.

Tycoch Square after a heavy snowfall, 1984.

Eastside Carnival fun at Maesteg Park, St Thomas, 1976.

The drinking font lamp which stood in the north eastern corner of Swansea recreation ground, adjacent to the west wall of St Helen's sports ground, 2005. Shortly after it was smashed by contractors working at the spot. It was originally sited there in 1887 when Victoria Park was opened to celebrate Queen Victoria's Golden Jubilee and when the recreation ground was bequeathed to the citizens of Swansea. The lamp now lays in two pieces at the museum stores in Landore.

FRIENDS OF SWANSEA CITY FOOTBALL ASSOCIATION

500

WNO 484

This open top bus was just one of the many vehicle that took part in Swansea's first ever Lord Mayor's parade.

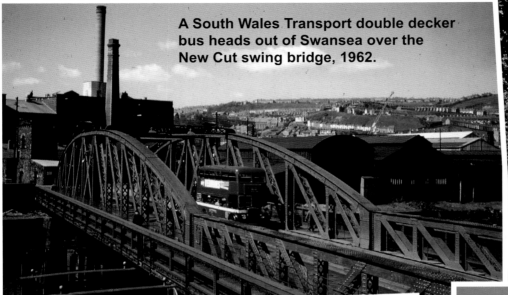

A South Wales Transport double decker bus heads out of Swansea over the New Cut swing bridge, 1962.

The former Swansea Guildhall, 1956.

A farmer harvesting potatoes in a field at Pennard.

St Mary's Church, late summer, 1959.

Tower block flats at Clyne Court, Sketty Park, mid-1960s.

Erecting the Big Top for Chipperfield's Circus at the Recreation Ground, Brynmill, early 1980s.

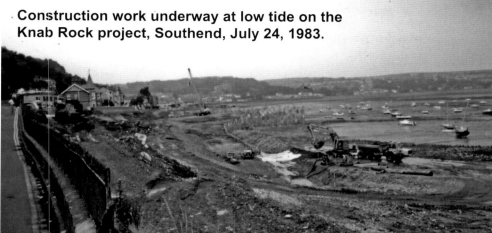

Construction work underway at low tide on the Knab Rock project, Southend, July 24, 1983.

Exhibitors in one of the cattle classes at the Gower Show, Penrice, August 2, 1979.

A religous procession headed by participants bearing a heavy wooden cross climb Morris Lane, St Thomas, early 1970s.

The reception class at Clase Infants School, 1981.

CLASE
INFANTS SCHOOL
SWANSEA
1981
RECEPTION 7

Olchfa School senior netball team, 1981.

Members of the 20th Swansea 1st Morriston Scouts, winners of the Scout sports day held at Clase School, 1984.

Beaujolais night at the Welcome Inn, Mynyddbach Common, 2000.

A single deck tramcar prepares to leave the terminus, High Street, 1910.

The Co-operative store at Lewis Street, St Thomas, 1959.

Mumbles Road, near Sketty Lane, 1959.

Chapter 7

Taking a
Break

A group of children and their parents all set for a day trip on a Habberfield coach in 1948.

Taking a paddle in the sea off Swansea Beach, 1906.

Crowds fill the sands at Swansea, near The Slip, with the bridge and the Guildhall clock tower in the background, late 1940s.

A group of Swansea women in a charabanc on a Mothers' Day trip, 1925.

A family group on the beach near Sketty Lane, 1922.

Caravans have certainly come a long way! These were in use at a caravan park on the hill into Caswell. No doubt though they provided many people with a well earned break in 1951.

The annual works outing of the Swanmet Engineering Company based at Morriston. This trip was to Aberdare Park in the early 1950s.

A Swansea family holiday at Butlins Pwllheli, 1954.

Male members of staff of JT Morgan's store on a summer outing to Tenby in the 1960s.

Terrace Road Mens' Guild on an outing to Symond's Yat, 1966.

A brother and sister enjoy the fun of the roundabout at Blackpill Lido, August 1966.

A group of St Thomas and Foxhole Road residents on a trip to Blackpool, 1955.

A Tir John Power Station staff outing to Worcester in the early 1950s.

These Swansea lads on a trip to Jersey in 1951 had just emerged as the winners in a tug of war contest.

On the beach at Langland, with the bathing huts and Convalescent Home in
the background, early 1960s .

A group of Trallwn and Llansamlet friends and neighbours on holiday in Italy 1960.

Members of the Mens' Guild of Terrace Road Chapel on a day out to Glastonbury, 1967.

Ponies and their riders cool off in the sea at Swansea Beach during July, 1969.

Members of the 42nd Fforestfach, Swansea Scout troop on a trip to Big Pit, Blaenavon, 1982.

Retired staff of the Ford Motor Company at Jersey Marine assemble in the plant's rotunda building before setting off on a day out, 1985.

A youngster gets up close to an owl during a birds of prey demonstration during a summer show at Singleton Park, 1987.

Soaking up the sun at Mumbles Pier, August 1967.

Young members of New Siloh Chapel, Band of Hope, all dressed up in their Sunday best before heading off for a special picnic at Port Eynon, Gower, 1955.

Enjoying a motor boat ride on the boating lake at Blackpill Lido, August, 1966.

Parents, children and friends from Gendros Mother and Toddler Group on a visit to Penscynor Wildlife Park, Cilfrew, Neath, June 27, 1989.

Members of St Michael's Church Youth Club, Manselton, on a walk at Ilston, Gower, Easter, 1989.

A family day out at Pembrey Country Park for staff of the Swansea branch of the Nationwide Building Society, August 2002.

Chapter

8

The boys and girls of class 1,
St Helen's Infants School, 1936.

Class 4, Oxford Street Infants School, 1915.

Pupils of Swansea Parochial School, 1907.

Pupils of the second class in Cwm Infants School, Bonymaen, with their teacher, 1920.

Standard 6, Oxford Street Boys' School, 1935.

Pupils of St Thomas Girls' Junior School, 1952.

Pupils of Cwm Council School, Bonymaen, 1913.

Class 1, Baptist Well Council Boys' Junior School, 1928.

A group of boys at Lloyds' School with their teachers, headteacher and even a dog, 1948.

Form 4, St Winifred's Convent School, 1950.

Pupils of Gwyrosydd School, Penlan, 1953.

All Saints' Church Junior School, Mumbles, with teachers Mr Williams and Mr Longhurst, early 1950s.

The Mayor and Mayoress of Swansea, Councillor and Mrs William Evans, visiting Dyfatty Infants School, 1955.

Students and staff at Swansea Training College, 1949-1951.

Form 1D, Dynevor School, with headteacher Meredydd Glyn Hughes, deputy headteacher Horace Griffiths and their form teacher Mr Jeff Hopkins,1960.

A group of girls at
Glanmor Girls'
School, 1950.

Form 6A Arts, Bishop Gore
Grammar School, 1956.

A class at Dunvant Junior School, 1961.

These recorder players provided some of the music at the St David's Day celebrations at Bishopston Junior School, 1971.

Class 4T, Penlan Multilateral School with teacher Mr Godsell, 1960.

A class at Cwmbwrla Junior School, on St David's Day, 1971.

Mrs Lorne's Class, St Helen's Infants School, 1967.

A class at Terrace Road Primary School, with their teacher, 1972.

A mixed class at Manselton Junior Comprehensive School, with their form teacher, 1972.

First year pupils at Bishopston Comprehensive School, 1975.

Pupils of Llwyn Y Bryn Girls' School present a copy of a new book, a Guide for Disabled People, to West Glamorgan County Council Chairman, John Allison, November 21, 1975.

Class J1, Arfryn Junior School, 1975.

Sixth form prefects at Llwyn Y Bryn Girls' School, 1976.

The reception class at Gendros Infants School, Armine Road, Fforestfach, celebrate St David's Day, 1980.

Pupils of Gendros Primary School with teachers Mr Andrews and Miss Bennett, 1982.

A class at Ysgol Gyfun Gwyr, 1989.

Pupils at Ysgol Gynradd Gymraeg, Lonlas, 1997.

Three classmates at Ysgol Gyfun Gwyr, 2000.

Chapter
9

An aerial view of Swansea Airport,
May 20, 1976.

On the
Move

The Mumbles Train passes houses on Oystermouth Road on its way back to Swansea, July 18, 1959. Swansea No. 2 signal box on the Central Wales Line is on the embankment.

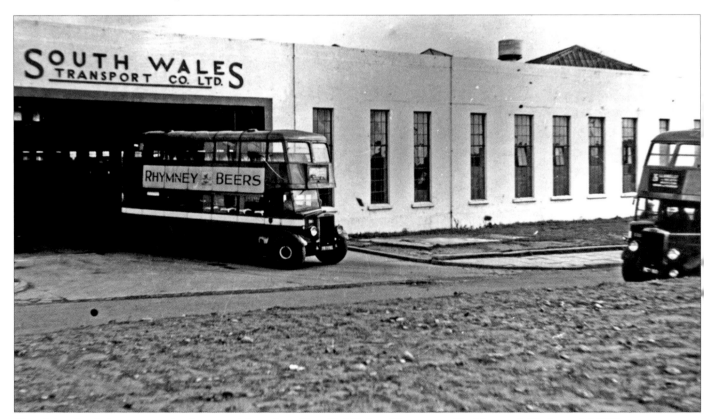

Double deck buses entering and leaving South Wales Transport's Ravenhill depot, 1950.

Tramcar 64 at the bottom of Wind Street, 1924. This was the terminus for double deck trams as they couldn't continue under the bridge.

An RAF launch at Swansea Docks, 1951. It had sailed from Pembroke Dock to tow back a Sunderland flying boat re-fueller. At the time Swansea Docks was the closest available for loading fuel.

A South Wales
Transport Leyland
double decker in
The Kingsway on
the 76 route from
Brynmill to Port
Tennant,
early 1950s.

Pontarddulais junction
railway station, looking
towards Llanelli, 1957.

Llansamlet North railway
station, looking towards
Skewen, mid-1950s.

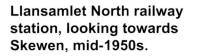

FFORESTFACH
CAEREITHIN
23 PENLAN

380

GWN 92

An AEC Regent III double decker alongside Castle buildings,
early 1952. This was one of the first eight foot wide vehicles
delivered to South Wales Transport a year earlier.

A tight squeeze in the lock for these three vessels, April 1964.

A British Rail diesel locomotive at the Maliphant sidings train-wash, 1967.

The Mumbles Train at its Rutland Street terminus, mid-1950s.

A horse-drawn brewery dray outside the Trafalgar pub, Oystermouth Road, 1964.

A young lad waits anxiously to board the Mumbles Train at the pier, ready for its return to Swansea, February, 1957.

One of South Wales Transport's, unpainted AEC double decker buses emerges from the company's Brunswick Street bus wash, 1960s.

Morris Bros coaches lined up outside Swansea Guildhall, 1960.

A new era for Swansea — the opening of Fairwood Airport, 1958.

A low loader vehicle carrying an earth moving machine operated by Morris Bros, outside the company's Ysgol Street, Port Tennant depot, mid-1960s.

A rescue truck and its crew at Swansea Airport, late 1970s.

Redundant railway locomotives in sidings at East Dock engine shed, August 1965. The condemned locos were stored here before being hauled away to Bird's scrapyard at Morriston for breaking up.

Pleasure vessels moored on the River Tawe including Coquet, a vessel owned by Henry Trollope, Commodore of Swansea Boating and Sub Aqua Club, 1980.

A lifesaving demonstration co-ordinating an RAF helicopter and the Mumbles Lifeboat, in the sea off Mumbles Pier, July 22, 1984.

An Air Wales aircraft at Swansea Airport, 2004.

Unloading operations underway at the King's Dock hoists, mid-1980s.

A diesel locomotive hauls a train of mixed freight wagons at Burrows Sidings. Danygraig engine shed is in the right distance. The photograph was taken from Burrows Sidings signal box, mid-1980s.

Chapter 10

A group of children and their parents at just one of the many parties held in Swansea to celebrate VE Day, 1945.

Parties and Parades

Residents of Wimmerfield, Killay, during their VE Day celebrations, 1945.

All dressed up for party time at the Heathfield Club, 1950.

Members of the 4th Swansea St David's Brownie pack during the 1953 Corpus Christi parade near the Slip Bridge. They were on their way from the church to St Helen's sports ground.

A group of Army Cadets on parade in the forecourt of Swansea Guildhall, St Helen's, June 1952.

The Christmas party at Swansea Council's Ynys-y-plant residential nursery, Mumbles Road, West Cross, 1953. The nursery is now a block of flats.

A group of Manselton churchgoers who attended the Festival of Wales parade at Cardiff, 1958.

A Band of Hope group passes the Globe Inn, Landore, during a Whitsun procession, early 1900s.

Some of the staff of Brown Brothers Motor Factors, Fforestfach industrial estate, at a
Christmas Party, 1967.

Staff gather for a presentation to mark the retirement of Irfon Bowen as manager of Barclays Bank,
Morriston, 1970.

Staff of dental suppliers Cotterill & Co, Walter Road, with their partners at a Christmas party, 1972.

Crowds gather in The Kingsway when the circus arrived in town and paraded some of its animals to draw attention to its presence, late 1960s.

One of the floats that took part in Swansea Carnival, July 1973.

Youngsters of the congregation of Hill Chapel, North Hill, dressed for a concert, mid-1960s.

Swansea City fans follow the open top double decker bus that carried their team on a victory parade around the city after winning promotion to the First Division, 1981.

Decorated floats set off from the car park at Bracelet Bay, to take part in Mumbles carnival, July 30, 1983.

Residents of Aberdyberthi Street, Hafod, celebrate the Royal Wedding of Prince Charles and Lady Diana, July 29, 1981.

Mothers and children of Ullswater Crescent, Bryn Rock, Morriston, during a street party to celebrate the Royal Wedding of Prince Charles and Lady Diana, July 29, 1981.

Chapter 11

The chimneys of Hafod copper and silver works reach for the sky among the industrial smog of the lower Swansea Valley, 1890. All that remains of this scene is the clock tower, visible from the nearby Landore Park and Ride station.

Hard at
Work

The Mond Nickel Works, Clydach, 1925.

Brynmill Infants School was used as a hospital during the First World War. The wounded soldiers seen here with nursing staff in December 1918 are wearing hospital blues as they were known.

Some of the women who made jerry cans at Cwmfelin works during the Second World War.

Employees of Cwmfelin Steelworks June 19, 1937.

A group of female employees of Marks & Spencer, Oxford Street, on the roof of the building 1938.

Some of the firing kilns at Swansea Brickworks, mid-1940s.

Employees of Swansea Brickworks mid 1940.

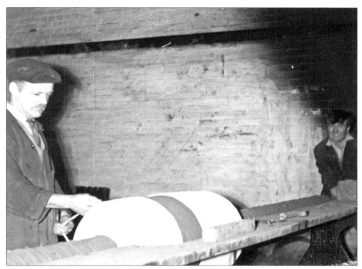

Workers at the Millbrook engineering works, Landore, 1960.

Bill Spinks, a Customs officer at Swansea Docks, 1951.

Swansea County Borough Council employees outside the Guildhall, 1946.

Operators at work in the GPO Swansea telegraph office, early 1950s.

Employees of the mechanical maintenance section of the Bernard Hastie sheet metal works on a visit to Margam Steelworks, Port Talbot, to view its new strip mill, 1952.

The crew of RAF launch Pinnace 1277, having a well earned tea break while at Swansea Docks collecting fuel for Sunderland flying boats based at Pembroke Dock, 1951.

Construction of the basement of the tinning lines at Velindre Tinplate Works, September 30, 1950.

Employees of the
Royal Insurance
Company's office,
Caer Street, 1959.

Staff outside B & J Pressdee's bakery shop at 135 Mumbles Road, Mumbles, 1960s.

The opening team of the Dragon Hotel, Belle Vue Way, in the hotel's former ballroom, May 12, 1961. Mr Hugh Gault, manager, is in the centre of the front row.

A group of Swansea railwaymen take a break from their labours, 1961.

Composing room staff at the South Wales Evening Post shortly after the newspaper's move to their new Adelaide Street offices, 1968.

Washing down a bulk tanker at the Mobil gas bulk depot, Trewyddfa Common, Plasmarl, 1961.

Technicians involved in building the scientific test rig at Sketty Hall, while working for the British Iron and Steel Research Association establishment there, 1962.

Some of the staff of the Dolphin Hotel, Whitewalls, 1963.

Head cook Nellie Clement-Floyd of Manselton, with the canteen staff at the Aluminium Wire and Cable Company works, Fabian Way, early 1960s.

Soldiers from 108 Field Squadron, Royal Engineers, practising on the short range at the Drill Hall, Richardson Street, 1964.

Easton Bros
scrap yard, The
Strand, 1964.
Inset: owner
Walter Easton.

Earthmoving
operations
underway during
construction
work at Singleton
Hospital, 1969.

The electric brush finishing workshop at Morganite Carbon, Morriston, 1969.

This is all that remained of the once mighty Hafod Copper Works in 1986. The works was established by the Vivian industrial family in the early 1800s.

Chapter 12

Participants in Swansea Grammar School's 6.5 mile senior cross country run, 1948.

Some good Sports

Bishop Gore Grammar School's First XV, with Mr DL Walters, Physical Education teacher, and Dr. Ellis Lloyd, Headmaster, 1956-57.

Sketty Rugby Club XV, 1919-20.

Members of Brynmill School shinty team, 1938.

A Sketty RFC squad with officials, 1919-1920 season.

Danygraig School cricket team, summer 1948.

A lone sea fisherman enjoys his sport on the beach at Horton, 1975.

Three of 1948's sporting finest — John Jones of Danygraig; Jim Pressdee of Oystermouth and G Harris of Townhill. Jim Pressdee went on to make his name on the cricket field for Glamorgan and later in South Africa.

The Welsh contingent who took on England at St Helen's in an NCB rugby international, April 22, 1950.

The 'Swansea Irish' bowls team after winning the locally held internationals, 1950.

Port Tennant Stars who were Swansea Senior League Cup finalists for six years running 1953-1960.

Players and officials of St Joseph's senior first XI 1955.

The bowls team of Richard Thomas & Baldwin's Landore works, 1956.

Manselton School rugby team, 1960-61 season with their teacher and headteacher.

Members of Danygraig Primary School Parents' Association who took part in a charity football match at Maesteg Park, St Thomas, 1966.

Members of the cricket team of Lloyds Bank, Swansea, after playing a game at Cheltenham, June 18, 1961.

The Ragged School youth soccer team at Ashleigh Road playing fields, 1967.

The boys of Powys Avenue School, Townhill, rugby team, 1961.

Members of Terrace Road Mens' Guild enjoy a game of cricket during a day out to Symond's Yat in the Wye Valley, 1966.

Sporting presenter David Parry Jones commentating on a cricket match from the rooftop at St Helen's ground, August Bank Holiday, 1960.

Cooneys Playboys — members of the darts team at the Coppermans pub, St Thomas, 1960.

The boys of Powys Avenue School Townhill football team, 1962-63 season.

**A hang glider soars into the air
off Rhosilli Down, July 24, 1979.**

Swansea Harriers senior mens' team early 1970s. Included are Welsh rugby internationals Alan Martin and JJ Williams.

Teacher Phillip Andrews with the rugby team at Gendros Primary School, early 1980s.

Members of Swansea Sub Aqua Club prepare for a diving training session, 1980.

The rugby squad of Gendros Primary School, Fforestfach, with teacher Mr Andrews, 1981.

One of Olchfa School's successful netball teams 1981.

Members of Darwin's Squash Club, Morriston, during a presentation evening, 1984.

Participants from Swansea show off the trophies they won at a BT golf tournament in Tenby, 1985.

Physical education teachers at Olchfa School, 1985.

Members of the City of Swansea Swimming Club with chairman Gwyn Powell, left, 1991.

Members of Parc Llewellyn Bowls Club who won the Swansea Bowls Association Dillwyn Shield final, 1990. They are: left to right: J Scully, V Davies, P Harris and B Harris.

Riders in the Kellog's cycle tour race at the junction of Craddock Street and The Kingsway, August 1993.

The cross country team of Ysgol Gyfun Gwyr who were West Glamorgan Champions, 1993-94.

Members and officials of
Swansea Acrobatic Club
during a visit to Mannheim,
Germany, August 2000.

John Charles CBE with
Sir Stanley Matthews
at a charity fund raising
gala 1990.

Skiers on the
dry ski slope,
Morfa, 1999.

Members of Swansea Acrobatic Club, 2000.

Crowds lined Constitution Hill to witness the Kellog's Tour of Britain cycle race, 1993. The hill, one of the steepest in the city, was used as a special stage in the event.